LIBERAL CHIC

KAREN KELLOCK PH.D.

**Manual for
Superior Men**

**A complete theory based on Einstein physics,
Political Psychology, Systems Theory
and Archetypal Psychiatry.**

**FORMULA
All success attraction
All disease obstruction
All recovery elimination**

**You must fast on all three
OBSTRUCTIONS:
People
Habit
Food**

LIBERAL CHIC

The sacred home was protected from evil influences but now pornography comes right in and we're defenseless. From our lovely home and starry nights with happy sounds and beautiful sights, suddenly it was HELL, alright?   Betrayal Trauma: a deeply distressing or disturbing experience caused by infidelity, affairs or betrayal.   The spiffy slut with high degrees never gets the respect she needs, the well dressed beta male with no morals or love of the Lord: you admired him girl.   To move forward we revisit the past with a new view: we went no contact in order to bloom.

TOO BUSY FOR YOU

RELENTLESS CYCLE OF DISCARD
FRIENDS OUTRAGEOUS AUDACITY
REJECTION BRINGS ON CORRECTION
CHILDHOOD WOUNDS & PEOPLE PLEASING
NARC ABUSE GLOSSARY
HEALING TAKES *ENERGY*
THE PAST LOOKING GROSS
THE TRUTH IS CALLOUS
STAY MUTE ON INTENT
DON'T WANT YOU ANYMORE
PEOPLE BARNACLES
JUST CONTINUE EXPANDING
IGNORE BEAUTIFUL STORIES
THE JEALOUS IDLE
KEEP HAVING FUN ADVENTURE
RESIST THE BORROWERS
SEX SIN HAS BEEN NORMALIZED
DENIAL ABOUT FRIENDS
FIGHTING FOR RIGHTS TO SIN
WE WANTED FRIENDS
GROSS INVASION NUMBNESS
SKINNY AND WINNING
SOLITARY GENIUS

TOO BUSY FOR YOU

It makes her feel superior to discard you like an old shoe. You gotta face she felt better than you.

The truth: Whenever people tell you they're too busy it just means you have low priority honey.

RELENTLESS CYCLE OF DISCARD

Don't go back in: don't start the relentless cycle of valuing, devaluing and then discarding.

Reaching out would be the greatest mistake cuz the situation stays the same/they won't change.

They win when you lose. That's how it is so they must make you lose so they can win Sue.

You didn't just grow apart. They actively put you down, isolated & falsely compared you with others.

You get up, they want a piece of the action which is taking you down--which is their supply son.

Guard your pets from the nasty rat: walk away GENTLY and be as nice as you can be see--protect.

Be sweet and keep sweet for the sake of your pets cuz if he's angry at you it's THEM he targets.

FRIENDS OUTRAGEOUS AUDACITY

You don't need those people but think you do cuz constant chaos lowered your self-esteem Sue.

The groupie thing drove me crazy cuz it wasn't my generation: we were into the individual son.

TOO BUSY FOR YOU

The outrageous audacity to bring all their friends to your house as if entitled to--it was gross.

When you're up you get insults, when you're down you get pep talks: that's how they control us.

Anyone who can bring you up can easily bring you down so become impervious to manipulations.

Unless they can control you they can't control themselves: that's how his mind works sis.

As the trauma bond persists you want him more then his drunkenness is worse than ever before.

Because he admires/wants what you have, his lovebombing is overwhelming and you're glad.

See who you are, he wants your star. But give into it one inch and he'll dump you just like before.

REJECTION BRINGS ON CORRECTION

Don't think back to when you were used. At your new heights this acts as an anchor below Sue.

Don't get involved again or the awful hurt may last decades this time son. Poking a bear is no fun.

We must educate the youth on REJECTION or look at the ramifications at the best's destruction.

Some idiot loser rejected me outa jealousy and it took decades to get back to emotional sanity.

I never stopped thinking about him or lurking until he died and then I was strangely relieved, aye.

If you have early trauma [abandonment] as an infant then subsequently all of life is corrective.

TOO BUSY FOR YOU

Someone rejects you and you want him MORE with a craving/addictive fire that's truly hardcore.

Depending on the energy and intensity of the animal that inverted craving becomes unstoppable.

CHILDHOOD WOUNDS & PEOPLE PLEASING

To heal from narc rejection you must heal childhood wounds: were you a people pleaser Sue?

A narc wants one who doesn't know about narcissism or hasn't healed from things done to them.

It almost killed you emotionally but stripped you of resources. If not money it's the TIME loss.

Don't be on the rollercoster of emotions any longer. Now you're in control if done with that loser.

Learning about the narcissist is the highway of self-empowerment like never before son.

The pinnacle of indifference is a most attractive place to be girl, the charm of a greater world.

Maybe he wants to get married again but your healing took too much work to EVER go back in.

NARC ABUSE GLOSSARY

Narc abuse cycle Glossary: object constancy, rage fits. rejection without closure, not giving a shit.

See also gaslighting, stonewalling, silent treatment, triangulation, blame-shifting, shapeshifting.

You know all this stuff now--my God how you know it--and have healed, a lot of work for growth.

TOO BUSY FOR YOU

So don't go back. See what you went thru--the gravity of it: how I wish someone had told me that.

You had a light bulb moment, studied the syndrome to the end and have been thriving ever since.

As an empath pleaser you didn't want the relationship to end & did what you could to make amends.

Don't go back, you shouldn't accept the hoover. You're getting so much better and they're losers.

HEALING TAKES *ENERGY*

Healing takes ENERGY so you can't foolishly expend it on the narcissist and his flying monkeys.

He lures you in and you get closer and closer until you don't know how to detach yourself ever.

They want you to want them again so they can not reciprocate to what you want: forget em.

Don't let em get their supply from watching you crumble and fall into despair: beware.

Everything they're about is setting you up for disappointment. Stay separate/happy woman.

THE PAST LOOKING GROSS

Being older and wiser of course things look grosser and meaner as you look back at your behavior.

Don't worry about this, it's just a little blurp in the universe and people couldn't care less.

You didn't do what they said you did & that's all that matters--now build your tiny home instead.

TOO BUSY FOR YOU

Go beyond human society cuz you came in alone and go out free of every parasite you've known.

Be happy: go camping, start painting, totally do your own thing and never go back to that fling.

So happy in a life of new endeavors as all that hurt energy goes into an exciting inner adventure.

THE TRUTH IS CALLOUS

Cuz people are cruel and he/she was the cruelest. Face it, stop submerging it: the truth is legit.

This wonderful journey of self-discovery is actually just reclaiming your lost identity--be happy.

Loveboming does not indicate better behavior towards you but needing you or a distaste for solitude.

Narcissists are so without empathy that's why they can leave you suddenly without a word see.

If he had a better offer he'd leave you in an hour. See instability: scary but essential for clarity.

Don't hang your hopes on anyone even if you're begging or taking care of em. They could change man.

Once you see their devaluation/turn go inside to the quiet stoic mode you've already learned.

STAY MUTE ON INTENT

When you voice your intent to depart be ready for a whirlwind of emotional chaos: be smart.

If alert you'll see devaluation as it happens. Buck up, go inside, love yourself and make plans.

TOO BUSY FOR YOU

It's over, just like that. Hard to believe cuz you're a person with object constancy--it's sad.

Sudden unplanned departures and separations are horrible but you gotta buck up now girl.

You didn't plan it nor did you warrant it. It's just how the narcissist is set up but later he'll pay up.

People are so cruel when they got nothing to lose and you trusted right away like you do Sue.

DON'T WANT YOU ANYMORE

Something happens and they just don't want you anymore Sue. They feel better than you.

They're like a cold pet owner who casually gives his dog away then wants him back later ok.

They have no object constancy: they can't keep their heart on you if there's no gain for them see.

Withdraw all energy/focus on people and put it all on you now. They'll hurt you if you don't.

Be careful cuz facades of composure can change quickly and he'll look like a monster/ugly.

Accept the everchanging fluidity of life. You may be alone now but it all changes when free of strife.

She's gone, he's gone. People come and go but God is always here along with angels all around.

PEOPLE BARNACLES

You hung onto people like a barnacle and it was a sad thing you know but now you'll ignite/grow.

TOO BUSY FOR YOU

The world is full of narcissists who get off on ghostings & sudden rejections but you're onto them.

Don't ever go back in again, you owe it to your heritage, ancestors and God who created you son.

Make me proud by standing alone, not by needing people and acting so dependent & ingrown.

Men: get into building things. Women: get creative and write about feelings. Go right-brain: clarity.

Men don't want a needy clinger. Women: open to destiny/talents until the the right one enters.

JUST CONTINUE EXPANDING

Just continue to expand and develop 'til your husband recognizes you, determined to marry up.

"I just need time and space" means they have someone else lined up but need you to be there ok.

The hoover is the attempt of a toxic individual to draw one back into the vortex of control/tyranny.

The soul purpose of the hoover is to regain control. It's pure manipulation: give in and grow old.

How can the hoover be proof of love if they never loved you in the first place? Get real ok.

They're just seeing how far down they can push you for the sake of their own self-validation Sue.

Your desperation makes em feel cocky & confident but it's all a system: they'd go down if you were up.

When they see you're not miserable with their absence they will offer you a nice, sweet hoover sis.

TOO BUSY FOR YOU

Lure of a pit viper: telling you everything you want to hear and boasting they've changed for sure.

They just want the chance to get back in, in order to put you down again. They know you well friend.

IGNORE BEAUTIFUL STORIES

They have a beautiful story of how much they've changed & what you mean to them Jane.

Being victimized by users over and over is not godly but we think that way for some reason don't we.

You have boundaries, they don't. You have not ENFORCED them so they invade without a thought.

They borrow things, like a sorority wearing each other's clothes. It sickens you as they encroach.

You have high boundaries cuz you're superior baby. Hold your head up high/they're disgusting.

They're social and don't have those boundaries. They'll bite on each other's apple, you won't see.

THE JEALOUS IDLE

People who've worked hard for what they have build high walls and not cuz they're selfish at all.

It's cuz the angry idle wanna come and get some: to hang out/be entertained/take your mon.

Genius is 99% hard work Einstein said. When you've finally succeeded they all wanna be fed.

Just cuz you live somewhere doesn't mean you gotta be chummy with the neighbors. Go inside sir.

TOO BUSY FOR YOU

It takes so much energy resisting people/enforcing boundaries it's just easier to be alone see.

Narcissists love to see people snap. They'll drive you to your limits and you won't like it like that.

You don't know your limits til you've dealt with the likes of them. You think you have but no ma'am.

If you're in a good place and know who you are, keep it like that cuz he'll want you back to torture.

If you haven't seen him or gone to his page you're forgetting about him: keep it that way.

KEEP HAVING FUN ADVENTURE

Keep having your fun/adventures/learning/partaking in things of value and you won't want Mr. Cruel.

The best way to control your husband is to do the housework excellently and be a lady.

Be the grade of person you want HIM to be then he'll fall in love/be with that upgraded image see.

The best way to control a husband is learn how to make the best pot roast with all day aromas ma'am.

Take interest in kitchen, learn how to please him: that's the old fashioned way marriages were lastin'.

RESIST THE BORROWERS

Don't lend things out cuz it's a mental hazard. Always thinking about it or begging to get it back.

The borrowers have now conquered your mind. There's a band between you and them now, aye.

TOO BUSY FOR YOU

Our phones buzz with notifications yet our hearts yearn for real connections but never get em.

The true gospel calls for repentance but the false one says you're forgiven without any changin'.

It calls you "loved" having God's mercy but not for you to carry your cross/crucify your flesh see.

It's not easy to give up those precious sins but much harder to endure the consequences friend.

SEX SIN HAS BEEN NORMALIZED

Sex sin has been normalized by the devil and society so we must separate ourselves to be happy.

Subtle deception is rife: They have a form of godliness without really striving to be Christlike.

Don't wait for the battle to get ready. The bible calls us to readiness not racked with shame/guilt see.

Be ready for subtle deception and knowing that MOST call evil good and good evil--and it's growing.

If ensconced in a bad past you can't be ready. You gotta prepare by wiping the slate clean daily.

BELIEF should lead to change, not hanging on to the deranged. Wake up to "friends" [an outrage].

DENIAL ABOUT FRIENDS

We push things under the rug with people--going dense to evil--but then it pops up in other avenues.

I'd get worse than them, that's what always happened. Many times it's sinners breaking connection.

TOO BUSY FOR YOU

It was like I was the evil one. But a triple Pisces takes on other entities if not well boundaried son.

People are cruel and in mal-adapting we may become cruel. This human pattern explains the world.

But all this great human understanding doesn't matter. You still gotta get em out along with chatter.

FIGHTING FOR RIGHTS TO SIN

People fight for the right to sin and it's serious. They'll believe anything to continue the ridiculous.

Whether it's abortion or social drinking when you should be abstaining, people justify anything.

Picture them as a mud surge where you can't stay clean in a bad association [need people purge].

You wanna be with them, remembering the good ol' days of partyin' but here demons are treading.

If they want something they'll justify it with the frontal cortex [and going by the book is dangerous].

Christians know that baby started as a design in God's mind and ending that blocks all mankind.

People love their sins so much they'll do anything to shut you up and you'll even go to prison brah.

WE WANTED FRIENDS

You wanted friends and you wanted to believe in them! You did everything son but the demons won.

Now you can't go amongst them because God said you'd end up just like them in the end.

TOO BUSY FOR YOU

They wouldn't leave me alone so in the desert I just bit my tongue and let em in, the evil throng.

They splashed in drunk at midnight demanding I fix tacos. I got thru it but feel PTSD even now.

It was like I didn't even exist, they could do anything to me and it was simply hateful to resist.

I had to be re-made on the Potter's Wheel to get a spine of steel and to make my boundaries real.

GROSS INVASION NUMBNESS

To handle gross invasions I just went numb, anticipating solitude later. I was a weak elder.

People will use you up as water seeks its own level and stealing [e.g. your time] is inherent to the devil.

I came from a sheltered background with alcoholism and thus had **NO** spine against social fascism.

I just wanted to please, just so they wouldn't insult me or continue to make my life miserable see.

This is a tear-jerker to anyone who's been thru it, they know the deep emotions running the gamut.

SKINNY AND WINNING

She was in her fifties, a big mean woman who targeted me--all cuz she was fat and I was skinny.

I became aware at age ten that when I was thin I was a dynamo but when heftier I was miserable.

I became aware at twenty that constipation was my biggest enemy as it stopped all creativity.

TOO BUSY FOR YOU

I gotta be a clear energy field as creativity comes **THROUGH** so obstruction isn't cool.

Picture the Drano ad: fruit keeps things clear, free and running so I see it as essential for happy.

Fruit and meat is the highest diet. Antioxidants plus essential protein & fats-- even if you fry it.

Of course I weigh every day like a jockey. Superfluity is our constant enemy so I keep it down see.

As a vegan my skin went to hell without animal protein. I added cheese but then it had to be meat.

Without protein it's Kwashiorkor the African disease: swollen with no energy/immunity/good skin see.

I always feel better after animal protein as it fixes all problems. Funny how they put it all down.

SOLITARY GENIUS

Solitary genius: Go to your email once a day and turn off all notifications on phones to escape.

While they were out there partying I was in here working, tirelessly and all night long see.

The problem: you get addicted to people texting you, self-esteem degrades and that's it Sue.

Be a genius, not a would-be. Go inside your own world and de-addict from this people worshipping.

Get your emails once a day and turn off notifications, I dare you. This is the test of discovery Sue.

Sagacity is the ability to be terse, laconic and wise. Not a lot of words but truth ringing in the skies.

LIBERAL CHIC

BAD INTENTIONS
BORROWING MONEY
WRONG INTENTIONS
BORN EVIL AND IMMATURE TOO
OLDER WOMEN ARE PAYING
ISOLATION AND VULNERABILITY
NOTICE CONTRADICTIONS
RICH WIDOWS GOING LOW
FLIP FLOP THEN DISCARD
FLATTERY IS CAMOUFLAGE
NEIGHBORS UP TO NO GOOD
BEING MISCAST OR AN OUTCAST
INTENTIONAL ENTANGLEMENTS
TO MOVE FORWARD SEE THE PAST
TERROR OF FALSE ACCUSATION
HORROR AT LOOKING BACK
EVIL CHILDREN ARE CRUEL
THE PAST IS LIKE AN ONION
LEARN TO SEE THRU PEOPLE
THEY DID THE BEST THEY COULD?
DO PEOPLE MAKE YOU SICK?
"D DAY": THE DAY OF DISCOVERY
COMPULSIVE <u>ABUSIVE</u> SEXUAL <u>RELATIONAL</u> DISORDER
BE HARDLINE—OR IT'S A LITTLE HERE, A LITTLE THERE
THE POWER OF SEX IS A HEX
RELATIONAL ABUSE IS INTEGRITY PROBLEMS
ATTACHMENT TRAUMA/BROKEN BONDS
GASLIGHTING IS CLASSIC: YOU'RE TO BLAME
GASLIGHTING ERODES YOUR REALITY
ISOLATION IS AUTOMATIC
EVIL SPIRITS RUIN HAPPY HOMELIFE
COPING TECHNIQUES OF BETRAYED WIVES
INTEGRITY PROBLEM IS BASIC
NORMALIZING SEXUAL ACTING OUT
MALE ENTITLEMENT TO SECRET SEX LIFE
COMPARTMENTALIZED SEXUALITY
MUST SEE YOU ARE A VICTIM

LIBERAL CHIC

RECOGNIZING TRAUMA
THE COLD REALITY
TWO CHOICES: ACCEPT IT OR DIVORCE IT
INTERVENTION IS INTERRUPTION
MINIMIZING IS BASIC: BE READY FOR IT
LIBERALISM IS RELAXED/NO MORALS
SECRET SEX WORLD WHILE IN A RELATIONSHIP
WRITTEN SMUT: EROTICA, "MOMMY PORN"
GASLIGHTING ERODES HER REALITY
A BETRAYED WIFE IS AN ABUSE *VICTIM*
SECRECY IS A COMPARTMENTALIZED MISTRESS
CARTOONISH SEXUALITY OR SWEET ELEGANCE?
HE USES SEX DISORDER TO ABUSE OTHERS
THINK OF THE. BETRAYED/TRAUMATIZED WIVES
LYING: PROCRASTINATING, INCOMPLETION
MEN IN THERAPY KNOW THE GRAVITY
BEATEN UP BY THE SAME PERPETRATOR
THE LOSER MENTALITY HAS A STINK
PORN AND DISORDER
BETRAYED WIFE TESTIMONY: MARIA
BROKEN BETRAYED WIVES, UNITE
SEX ADDICTION
TRUST IS A FABRIC THRU EACH CELL
NOT ABOUT HIM/SEX BUT BROKEN TRUST
ACROSS AMERICA HOMES ARE DESTROYED
NO WIFE CAN COMPETE WITH THE INTERNET
HIS PERSONALITY WAS SPOTTED
HE WAS EVERYTHING TO ME
ADDICTION: DESPITE MAJOR LOSSES
BETRAYAL TRAUMA IS PRIMAL PANIC
FIGHT—FLIGHT--FREEZE
WHO CAN I TRUST NOW?
EMOTIONAL TUG OF WAR
BETRAYAL TRAUMA SOOTHERS
STILL IN TRAUMA
COMMENT BY BETRAYED WIFE
TRUST AND RELATIONAL INTEGRITY/FIDELITY

LIBERAL CHIC

BAD INTENTIONS

Bad intentions: He keeps you chasing promises and assumptions, never consistent or solid, numb.

She can know she's chasing when she's consumed about him but not herself unfortunately.

She losing herself in order to attain someone else-- chasing assumptions that are obviously false

Strung out for years with no guarantees: what a sad plight for women due to low self-esteem.

She has babies but still she has no ring. That's the sad and sorry state of the traumatized see.

Now you have grandchildren but still no marriage. You've been strung so long you've managed it.

He keeps you chasing, pruning something that never produces promised fruit and always craving.

After six months kindly ask where it's going: Pin him down or cut him off and resuming dating.

He'll say for years "this is where I'd like to go" but a lady says no: what's your time frame Joe?

BORROWING MONEY

Gee he seems like a nice guy but he wants to borrow money. GIANT RED FLAG: Dump him honey.

He wants to borrow money, get you to co-sign, invest in his new business: block him/ghost him sis.

LIBERAL CHIC

James always came over on that day my money came and then that old pressure started ok.

Girl, you don't want a gigolo: a man who lives off of women. Times have changed? No they haven't.

Borrowing money is the biggest red flag of all. What a gigolo, he should be giving you money doll.

What a cheap, using, weaselly MISER you brought home sister. Get a real man or it's total disaster.

WRONG INTENTIONS

A man should be adoring and planning a life with you not seeing you as a financial option too.

Any man using you for finances is either too feminine to be your husband or a user to abandon.

It's a bad sign when men start asking women for money. A good man tries everything else see.

A good man will go out of his way to show he has no intentions of using her money/resources.

If a man is so small he asked a woman for money he is garbage to be thrown out all thru history.

If a man asks for money his intentions are off. He's not seeing you in the right away, he's a fraud.

He who guarantees a debt will surely suffer but he who declines is secure from hurt: remember!

All the men asking me for money instantly lost my respect for it's not how you treat an elect.

Basically losers see you as narcissistic supply and you can tell early exactly what kind of a guy.

LIBERAL CHIC

Only if living in the same household where finances benefit the lifestyle of both does this go.

If a good man has a business reversal he may not even tell her first, he'll exhaust everything else.

So you say due to feminism times have changed and men can borrow money from you dames?

BORN EVIL AND IMMATURE TOO

People are born evil and most never mature too. It's a wide path to hell but to heaven just a trickle.

Ok so the past was terrifying and humbling. Now let's review it positively, for there was so many.

Every time I expressed myself they acted scared and shocked like they wanted to lock me up.

God chose the most despised and mocked to fool the wise so it's beauty and riches after lies.

So not only are you an unpaid whore or sideline girl, now you pay him too? Ridiculous, an error.

I know a lot of you women are paying. Grown men asking you for money and you're caving.

Sickening: Ph.D. women paying for and being manipulated by grown men, I see it happening.

OLDER WOMEN ARE PAYING

A lot of you older women are paying. And as time goes on your paying more but soon he's leaving.

It's sad, ridiculous and unbelievable to me. You even act proud you're paying for your boy see.

LIBERAL CHIC

One clear set up is him isolating you from safe pillars but never introducing you to his world.

He severs you from all relationships then says "I'm God's gift to you" as he shovels shit.

ISOLATION AND VULNERABILITY

A woman isn't vulnerable until she's isolated. He gets her alone and then she sees his hatred.

Any man who hates those who love you has an agenda against you. Notice he's a sly whisperer too.

Like a preview that's far greater than the movie itself, a poser and joker came in and fooled you.

When there's little agreement between what he projects himself to be and reality you should RUN.

He keeps saying he's a lawyer but then why must he borrow your car? Notice disparities dear.

He's a millionaire but is very comfortable with others paying the bill all the time: notice examples.

The preview is syrupy sweet but the full movie is a terrifying disaster you will never repeat.

NOTICE CONTRADICTIONS

He's spiritual and loves God but his entire conversation is perverted and unwholesome, a fraud.

His life doesn't match his preview, something is just off. He's a hypocrite, common, a sneaky ripoff.

Wake up and realize "this guy is not what he's projecting". See the matrix then escape him.

LIBERAL CHIC

He brags he's strong but clearly seeks approval, he name-drops constantly which you see right thru.

You're a "strong woman", a liberal chic. But the way you are carrying on is very degrading I think.

She bought him a horse trailer and a new truck. He brought her ice cream the handsome chump.

RICH WIDOWS GOING LOW

First a rich widow he went thru all of it and left her with nothing in her old age fund: this is common.

You can't want sex that bad, to be made such a fool of and have to pay him, come on girl grow up.

Liberal chic: you actually left your nice husband for this, to be used and depleted and pissed?

A middle aged woman in a wet T-shirt contest. Give me a break, get some class witch and resist.

And as for you: you're clearly all about sex and I find it blasphemous so now I say: good riddance.

You talk about sex so blatantly to everyone, shit shots to hook em in to your sexual soul tie son.

Shit-shots are said to test response. You have so many women soul tied now it's ridiculous.

FLIP FLOP THEN DISCARD

He flip-flops after sex [discard ok] so when he hoovers for money you gladly pay to resume charade.

Hah: Women have money and newfound power so it's even a lark to be asked by a hat-in-hander.

LIBERAL CHIC

It even makes her feel more secure, enabling money dependency. It never works, the idea is lunacy.

Every woman wants to be desired, knowing her man is attracted to her but flattery gets creepy.

He flatters her to an uncomfortable extent. He's buttering her up but does she ever suspect?

FLATTERY IS CAMOUFLAGE

It's called rapid-fire flattery: His attempt to distract her from the radical danger he carries.

Good luck on this fruitless endeavor going nowhere. Don't give him card or let him drive your car.

You're paying for relationship otherwise. And nothing. is more disgusting in even a gigolo's eyes.

Needy silly women easily taken in are payin' cuz he starts innocently asking and she wants him.

She's easily taken in by her sons and her young lover who's just another boy at the house sir.

Every woman I talk to is paying. I'm not kidding, it's sickening. Feminism does it all: degrading.

She's so liberated she lets herself be used and even brags about her sexual chicness too.

All he's gotta do is flatter you. Flattery is a hunter's camouflage: it works every time with shrews.

By camouflage the hunter fades into the trees and grass and his flattery makes her ignore his crap.

Camouflage makes deer comfortable in the danger zone--so the hunter can shoot them dead.

LIBERAL CHIC

Flattery is love bombing and don't we eat that up as lovestarved victims of a generation's sinning?

When he flatters & loves you too much, yuk. See the signs cuz this type will reverse suddenly on ya.

Rapid flattery love bombing: he gets you on an ego trip to cut off common sense and discernment.

NEIGHBORS UP TO NO GOOD

A flattering neighbor is up to no good. He's priming to take advantage for sex, money or wood.

Bad intentions is always creating crises. He keeps your soul tied up in his drama at your expense.

It's his created drama. He's always laying plans while you're assuming all will be wonderful.

Esp. when you're wising up or he feels he's losing you he creates a crisis and makes it yours miss.

To him it's his situation. To you it's "our" situation as you fall into a bag of toxic love/adoration.

God's path is straight but a crooked path is circuitous from manipulations of fools among us.

The older wiser sagacious says: don't get involved. It's going down a rabbit hole lest you have love.

Via your toxic empathy you get caught up in his crises feeling so important, a virtue signaling nut.

BEING MISCAST OR AN OUTCAST

They never knew I had a Ph.D. nor had a Creative Act in me and truthfully treated me despicably.

LIBERAL CHIC

I felt what it's like to be disrespected and mocked--from that I learned more than a library of books.

Entanglements: his current crisis ties you up for months then when that simmers down, more fuss.

This guy above has bad intentions. He's demonic, diabolical, out to get you. Reject and go on.

This guy's toxic. He's intentionally entangling you cuz he knows your values, is setting you up too.

INTENTIONAL ENTANGLEMENTS

I had to go thru the ordeal of being disrespected and mocked to learn the psychology of kooks.

At some point lady you gotta wise up and say: "Not my problem, I'm outa here, have a good day."

God doesn't want you wasting your life with a man who never intended to do right by you, aye?

God doesn't want you giving time and money to a man who never even deserved a conversation.

I pray for every woman reading this: God give em the wisdom, confidence and courage to see a dis.

I pray you take control of your lives and to RECOGNIZE what it is you're dealing with dating guys.

The birds and the bees are chemistry but without values and boundaries you'll meet defeat see.

I pray you disencumber from users to put yourself in the position intended which is so far superior.

So you had a fatal mental disease, got caught up in a sin or was used as a trash bin: just start again.

LIBERAL CHIC

Let God's spirit pull you out of degrading or unfulfilling relationships now. I pray success for y'all.

TO MOVE FORWARD SEE THE PAST

To move forward we must revisit the past with a new view: we went no contact to BLOOM.

People are cruel and the world instructs them how. We can get over it tho' it seems impossible.

Because the abuser and her gophers always turns it around to where you're the crazy one.

A scapegoat system is the feeling you're not good enough and their only problem is you chump.

It's hard to face the little buddy you played ball with at four is your worst foe in the entire world.

As you grow so does their smear campaign in a desperate attempt to keep you below.

That's homeostasis in the dysfunctional system: maintaining the status quo, keeping you down.

Toxic siblings, narcissist abuse, unhealthy relationships mark early life before adequate boundaries.

TERROR OF FALSE ACCUSATION

Either you're nuts or it's all on her and she has to eat crow which she can never do you know.

Either you're nuts or they are and if you're sane all those things they said condemn em further.

In the face of her twisting facts, ignoring my good points and accusing me of THAT I shrank back.

LIBERAL CHIC

I wasn't used to having to defend myself. I felt drained of all creative inspiration, it was just hell.

Female thugs: When those women have a target they're like a pit bull who won't let go or give up.

As we unpeel the onion we see the roots of things and its obvious what before we didn't see.

Midlife this onion seems endless. I know I'll be reviewing stuff until my last breath for instance.

Suddenly you wake up as to WHO said what to WHOM thirty years ago and what followed soon.

Unless a world traveler from a toddler, what do we have but these family memories to review here?

Suddenly something jogs your memory and you're lost in reverie as it makes you angry or sad you see.

The victim is plagued with voices yelling inside. These are all uncovered as you unpeel, aye.

HORROR AT LOOKING BACK

I had memories putting me in horror of what I had conquered and risen above as a weak girl.

The horror of what I put up, who I let in, what I agreed to just to shut em up and who I called friends.

It's like our bodies were in a war living around narcissistic dysfunctional people, good Lord.

Somehow thank you God I survived the war but I have combat wounds in this unpeeling onion.

But wounds make me hypervigilant to disrespect and I get away/draw boundaries right away.

LIBERAL CHIC

These wounds are called PTSD and they haunt us constantly tho' the culprits got off free.

Even though he stole your furniture and good name he still embarked on a nasty smear campaign.

EVIL CHILDREN ARE CRUEL

Sibling abuse is a very scary thing cuz it's in hiding and you know how cruel children can be.

Hey girl this is something you're to get beyond not a thing you succumb to on and on.

It was a 3 ring circus yet I won cuz I walked away but they stayed despite a break with destiny.

Such a beautiful place, and yet getting involved with people I went down painful rabbit holes.

I can't describe the insanity that came out of betrayal trauma. Years of being out of grace, fallen.

Relax, all of your past abusers are either dead or stuck in California. God evens it out I tell ya'.

Don't worry cuz there was never any true memory just magnetisms of the moment we "see".

THE PAST IS LIKE AN ONION

Reviewing the past is like peeling an onion, each layer revealing a new memory [abuse problem].

The part of the onion when you had no boundaries will reveal the most horrors being so ego alien.

Abuse is proportional to personal boundaries. With lack of boundaries abuse increases see.

LIBERAL CHIC

When they accused me unfairly while saying I had no degree I lacked the skill sets to defend me.

We're not happy around the toxic, unstable, unhealthy, malicious, hurtful and manipulative.

I thought, I can't stand to be around these people for one more minute cuz I'm SICK God!

I'm physically sick in their presence so my old doctor said "people make you sick, accept this".

LEARN TO SEE THRU PEOPLE

Don't back into old age, looking at the past. Instead open up to God, angels, true friends at last.

Don't worry about them, people come and go. They're either dead or the walking dead below.

The well dressed slut with high degrees will never have the respect she needs, don't you see.

The well dressed professional beta male with no morals or love of the Lord: you admired him girl.

I couldn't stand him the minute he walked in. He didn't light up the room he put it down in doom.

Once having digested crap from the past now focus on just your situation now in happy retirement.

THEY DID THE BEST THEY COULD?

"He/she did the best they could" is what survivors say after forgiving abuse from the cruel/cold.

Face it and get over it, don't be crippled by the inability to accept and really see it: SS sibling shit.

LIBERAL CHIC

You were a victim of the Cinderella Syndrome and now you're an older wise woman with a crown.

I was very aware of his toxic presence. He zeroed in to criticize. I felt shamed/blamed/silenced.

An aura of shame, blame and classism resonated from their presence and I'm afraid I bought this.

It's not funny to be locked in a dark closet or held down and tickled, causing claustrophobic people.

She'd make sure someone else—not even her--gets your inheritance rather than you get it sis.

Tickle torture allows the culprit to torture while saying you're too sensitive or just can't kid.

DO PEOPLE MAKE YOU SICK?

I was nauseated by her presence as she gossiped about me to anyone within distance.

It was in the pit of my stomach. Trauma pierces our heart and soul and we literally feel crushed.

Life is hard when you have someone on your tail like this. With false accusation it's hell pits.

That a relative would hurt us/make us feel inferior in front of the whole world seems ridiculous.

To try to bring us down, steal our joy and rain on our parade isn't what you'd think of family.

Making things worse, people believe em since they ARE your family. it's a tragedy believe me.

They made me feel sad, mad and bad and I knew that wasn't normal cuz I had a life of my own.

LIBERAL CHIC

We need to continuously jog old memories to know WHY we went no contact/they are enemies.

One reason you went no contact is you never heard from em anyway, a contradiction in the brain.

People aren't God, they have hangups, sex is everywhere. Ladies, we've got to face this spiritual warfare.

The sweet little lady said "he's the one who divorced me, by his filthy disgraceful secret sex life": she was free.

Dishonesty cracks your whole world. Then you can't trust a thing he says again: this is betrayal girl.

"D DAY": THE DAY OF DISCOVERY

Just by a CLICK he ruined his life. Historically he had to have an affair to do that but now it's just a like.

The dishonesty, secrecy and vulgarity of the discovery sends women over the edge: TRUTHFULLY.

Let's look at the wife discovering this: Her entire world and reality is shattered like pre-psychotic shock.

Take your focus off the sex addict and put it on his wife who is in shock, devastated, dangerously depleted.

Especially when it's home life, you have everything together! But it's unequal yoke from the gutter.

You've been abused as much as being beaten up in a hospital. It's an ontological insight which is fatal.

You trusted deeply, primally--and was busted in the face for it and disgraced on top of it, no more naiveté.

By seeing the porn discovery as relational abuse, she can refuse to re-engage but just work on her self.

LIBERAL CHIC

COMPULSIVE <u>ABUSIVE</u> SEXUAL <u>RELATIONAL</u> DISORDER

Sex is so normalized that most clinicians just can't accept that pornography is a form of domestic abuse.

Sex addiction isn't just about the man but the domestic violence to the psych of it all--it is RELATIONAL.

Just because it's a book/cartoon/written doesn't mean it's not hurting, leading to habits/harmful obsessions.

Focus is on sex addict behaviors, not a clear diagnosis or labeling of the integrity abuse/relational conduct.

Integrity abuse: You trusted him, you relied on him, and now you've found....THIS??????? How can you trust?

It's called Compulsive Abusive Sexual Relational Disorder, not "Sex Addiction" anymore. It's abuse, sir.

The compulsive part is the sexual, the abusive part is the relational. It's a combo--see this then go.

Liberalism is relaxed morals: You see it in churchgoers, conservatives, everyone. Gotta take a hardline.

BE HARDLINE—OR IT'S A LITTLE HERE, A LITTLE THERE

For it's a little then a little more. We're talking about a powerful lure: Satan knows sex sells the herd.

Anything even loneliness would be better than living in thistles and bristles cuz you're into THAT.

Get support, join your community/neighborhood gals while you totally isolate him. He'll be gone.

Because woman, you can't live with that demon. Not and keep your dignity, no ma'am.

LIBERAL CHIC

Dad once said: "I worry when she's **NOT** slamming doors"--when she just went on to the future.

There comes a time when you'd better get offa that train cuz that gold ring won't come around again.

Get offa that ceaseless merciless cycle with him and join the living so you can get some work done.

THE POWER OF SEX IS A HEX

Now you be a **LADY**, and be the **OPPOSITE** to such a low brow pig and the **OPPOSITE** to his carnal past times.

It's not about "sex preferences" but actual, literal Relational Abuse. This view will change everything for you.

You'll start to review your past together before you knew. How you saw things then vs now: fast to review.

I am a science discoverer who has discovered something SO shocking, SO life-changing, so devastating...

Life is a personal discovery about your Self as God predesigned and passing tests we're assigned.

RELATIONAL ABUSE IS INTEGRITY PROBLEMS

"Don't hang your hopes on people they'll always disappoint"--words of my ancestor George.

And then on top of her shattered dreams, she's accused of being a dam codependent with his disgrace, seedy.

Relational abuse is **INTEGRITY** problems: remaining true, thinking of the other before you act like a dam fool.

It's a developing psych model: Sexual-Relational Behavior. It's a two-part problem: the sex part, the abuse part.

LIBERAL CHIC

By lunging at female clerks in front of me that wasn't a "sex" but an abuse problem, wow now I see it.

ATTACHMENT TRAUMA/BROKEN BONDS

Attachment trauma, broken bonds: wow it hurts but it's him who called it quits by looking at those chicks.

I want a stable homelife before I die, this isn't it. The computer reflects man's evil/no one thinks of the wife.

That you could bring that crap into our lives, our home. I thought it was all sacred to you, I'm blown away.

It's not that you have no control, it's that you want to hurt me in a Relational Abuse Compulsion related to sex.

GASLIGHTING IS CLASSIC: YOU'RE TO BLAME

The intentional psychological manipulation of another's gut instincts--that's what it was but now I've retrieved her.

The secret sex reality has already eroded the INTEGRITY of the family to exist, underneath you feel pissed.

Relational INTEGRITY is a fundamental, basic healthy attribute of a relationship. When it fails, life's shit.

If someone's chipping away at the integrity of that system, the results is diseases/pathologies start up.

Heck, the chance for healthy integrity to even exist is corrupted. He naturally hides it cuz he knows it.

To the porn addict life is exciting but the ordinary joys of life are not. It's all dulled to grays and rot.

Secondary trauma from religious leaders encouraging her to forgive without knowing the sickening depth.

LIBERAL CHIC

It's impossible to spend so much time/energy engaged in a behavior and be fully on board raising children.

Take your eyes off of his "sex addiction" and put em on your betrayal trauma--that's his destruction on ya.

GASLIGHTING ERODES YOUR REALITY

Gaslighting is a manipulation through persistent denial, misdirection, contradiction and lying.

Gaslighting is an attempt to de-legitimize someone or what they are saying. Don't argue, start learning.

Gaslighting is a REALITY distortion, a form of emotional abuse from mild to it most painfully extreme.

Porn effects in married women: intense emotion, disruption in core beliefs/trust, changed self-image.

Also, changes in her reality and a hypervigilance in new policing or investigative behaviors.

Policing behaviors are the hallmark of trauma: when the system's looking for a way out and feels hysteria.

ISOLATION IS AUTOMATIC

These women become isolated [68%], show abrupt changes in behavior or blames themselves.

After betrayal trauma even the social butterflies with positive family ties go into isolation to sort out lies.

Some women readily forgive this--heck they have their own collections of it--or feel pity for the addict.

Who can she reach out to, where can she find safe places to talk this through? Concentrate on this for now.

EVIL SPIRITS RUIN HAPPY HOMELIFE

LIBERAL CHIC

There are spirits in a happy orderly home. Routines that make it smoothly run. But THIS is hell full blown.

A person can be a billionaire in perfect health but be brought down by something like this in a minute.

Life changes suddenly from fame to shame but also from shame to fame. Be careful but learn about his game.

For its effecting men all over the globe. That's why work's so shoddy and there is no excellence or renaissance.

The subliminal signs were there before the discovery--I felt disorderly, I felt a little funny, I started questioning.

Mormon ladies turning to alcohol to cope with betrayal trauma: things get maladaptive suddenly for ya.

COPING TECHNIQUES OF BETRAYED WIVES

96% of wives of sex addicts wives report that discovering this was their "greatest traumatic event"/can't forget.

Betrayal Trauma is when someone we rely on and depend violates our trust in a critical way—a horrible day.

48% have moderate to severe PTSD. Then there's secondary trauma from others in the industry.

Secondary trauma is real. If we reach out and pastor is aloof or ignorant there is depression and suicidality.

Viewing pornography--using another's body for one's self--is a form of unrighteous dominion in your home.

The new books on sex addiction are all about betrayal trauma, away from the old codependency model.

It's the fact he took a chance on your marriage when he KNEW the bloody consequences--this really hurts.

LIBERAL CHIC

She's not mad at him, her whole world has shattered. Description of sex addict wives.

INTEGRITY PROBLEM IS BASIC

He stopped? But he still has an integrity problem and continues to gaslight, lie and deceive. Must see.

The sad thing is how he's brought down our home for good. For how can I go back once it's understood?

Therapists: If you're not treating the abuse problem you're ignoring the victim--untreated because unrecognized.

Not treating the victim and seeing this as pure **ABUSE** is a serious omission. Some even say "why not join him?"

The women they see are not identified as abuse victims because that isn't how they see themselves.

You're being abused--he's not just a good guy trying to get his innocent pornography viewing under control.

Just by explaining psychological/emotional abuse to them they start crying with relief, joyful at the revelation.

NORMALIZING SEXUAL ACTING OUT

As a society we don't view cheating and infidelity as domestic abuse at all. Many just laugh if off.

As a sick society normalizes sex abuse it's nearly impossible for a betrayed to find one to talk to.

Cheating--porn and infidelity--are patterns of sexual acting out and if normalized the wife loses clout.

When there is sex discovery many clinicians blame the partner or the relationship--hard to imagine this.

LIBERAL CHIC

They go into a "it takes two to tango" model that blames the relationship esp. the intimate partner or spouse.

Facing sex life as abuse helps her to get to a safe place especially mentally. It changes everything, really.

She's already confused. To not see it as abuse allows abuse to continue cuz gaslighting is the tool used.

It's gender pathology: a disease in how one is manifesting their gendered self in ideas, behaviors, selections.

If Jezebel acts a slut to be "cute" as Blanche in the Golden Girls, that's her gender identity as long as it works.

MALE ENTITLEMENT TO SECRET SEX LIFE

The unhealthy societal scripts taught to boys/men around entitlements despite rights of others in the system.

The idea of sex entitlement is molded into the concept of masculinity so they feel compelled to hurt us badly.

Even males who aren't misogynist take on these ideas just by being part of society. Well I'm sick of it honey.

He would sexually act out to temporarily inflate his gender esteem, his unhealthy self-worth. Inadequacy = girls.

One way of compensating/gaining gender esteem is to sexualize, conquer and gain attention of women.

Having a separate sex life is much a male tradition and norm. Sexual entitlement is encourage in the dorm.

Where have we ever heard that sexual infidelity is a form of domestic violence? Never, nothing, not a chance.

Broken ribs and nose are nothing to shattered dreams, bombed reality and sickening heartbreak, see?

LIBERAL CHIC

COMPARTMENTALIZED SEXUALITY

They absorb up sexual entitlement and are encouraged in deceptive compartmentalized sexuality—just think of it.

Having a secret sex life while in a family is a form of immediate but covert dominance and control.

His power comes from withholding information that if they knew they would take steps for self-protection.

Power of his Lying: If they knew they would respond in a way that advocates for their safety and well-being.

Get out: The sex abuser may feel power just from having a secret sex life that his family doesn't know about.

Just by having that separate sexual life he thinks like his father Satan: it's about control, power, dominance.

The men say in therapy that acting out (e.g. porn) gave them a sense of retribution [payback] and power.

Secret pornography to run to has a way of balancing what he is dealing with in relational power and control.

This is a call for all therapists to take a trauma-sensitive approach in dealing with wives of all sex addicts.

The co-sex and codependency models are a form of victim-blaming and you even see it in the church.

MUST SEE YOU ARE A VICTIM

Turn from women who say to put up with pornography. Turn from them, avoid em, they are the vermin.

Many advertise their trauma approach but they still use co-sex, codependency or a hybrid. Need MORALITY.

LIBERAL CHIC

If you don't see them as a VICTIM of sexual abuse then you'll never get to the root of trauma/stay obtuse.

Recap: It's not just the discovery causing the trauma but the PATTERNS of gaslighting, minimizing and lying.

RECOGNIZING TRAUMA

If you recognize the trauma you must recognize the abuse for they go hand in hand, not the co-sex false view.

Therapist: If you're TIMID about using the word "abuse" with porn addicts then you won't win in the end.

Gender pathology goes right along with sexual entitlement, believe me. And it's your end cuz it means SECRECY.

The ingrained sense of sexual entitlement automatically leads to abuse. Dear Lord it happened in high school.

RECAP liberal chic: Having a separate compartmentalized sexual life in a relationship is a form of abuse.

Take the spotlight off the men so sexually mean and put it on the wife and kids hemorrhaging behind the scenes.

The wimp clinicians are scared seeing the wife of the porn addict as a "victim". Don't believe me? try em.

Tho' they accuse you of "keeping the wife in the victimized state", see the falsehood and continue this way.

If you feel part of the problem you try being more loving, helpful, forgiving. No help, you still have the trauma.

If I'm not a victim but a co-conspirator then I can't get to safety, I have no answer to my situation.

Feminist therapists are the secondary trauma of having his sexual cheating trivialized, coaching her to silence.

LIBERAL CHIC

The healing has to be swallowing reality, which is there's been significant victimization--just face it.

Seeing this "independent strong woman" as a victim allowed me to get to safety, to set boundaries.

THE COLD REALITY

The cold reality: he's living a double life, gaslighting you if you confront it--saying it's not so despite evidence.

Secondary shame: I could have been more sexy, I could have managed the betrayal trauma, it's my fault man.

She is re-traumatized by questions like "did you stop sex after having kids?" or "you're emotionally unstable."

I'm done fighting to save something that just ends up hurting me. Rollercoaster emotions, betrayal, lies.

it's a high-anxiety trauma state of mistrust and no amount of "I love yous" will change it, his patterns were obvious.

Pornography: In all cases you must separate from the disgrace. You've been abused, keep that straight.

To gaslight is to homogenize: to the wife he says "we're all sinners and you're a sinner too" like it's all the same.

It's NOT all the same. You did nothing to deserve this nasty spirit invading your home/dashing your hopes.

TWO CHOICES: ACCEPT IT OR DIVORCE IT

When it seems endless she has two choices, accept it or divorce it—triggering more panic, powerlessness.

The sense of powerlessness is so overwhelming it's almost relieving to say: if I submit I'll have more control, ok.

LIBERAL CHIC

The sex addict fantasizes and disappears into the excitement and PURSUIT of sex, not having it.

Adrenalin, endorphins and neurochemistry gets stirred up with their fantasy-- the tired man LOVES that adrenalin.

They aren't genitally excited but by endorphins, mood triggers like serotonin/dopamine: the CHASE.

The sex addict uses his fantasy to shift his brain chemistry--to be in a different place emotionally.

It's the LEAD UP to the experience with searching and hunting that provides the high to the impotent guy.

Male sex addicts acting out with porn cuz they can't handle emotional disruption/challenges at all.

INTERVENTION IS INTERRUPTION

Without intervention there's no interruption: he continues to do what he does and you're hurt again.

You can't restore intimacy --being known fully--if trust is broken and you don't know what else he's done.

The hurt went so deep I can't eat. I'm on my second day of a five day fast to go higher while digging deep.

Hypnotized by their sex instincts women are persuaded to do very dark things. Crime couples not just flings.

How can you be intimate or feel safe, always thinking they'll likely return to their sexual behavior?

Get armed guards and gardeners not this lazy shifty loser who never lifts a finger cuz he's lost in smut.

MINIMIZING IS BASIC: BE READY FOR IT

LIBERAL CHIC

This is not a big deal, don't worry about this, you're way over-reacting--this is his classic **MINIMIZING**.

Partial Disclosure: He didn't have one affair, he had seven. He went to massage parlor 3x weekly, not 3 times.

It's always things like that--partial disclosure, denying, lying, minimizing, gaslighting. You keep prying.

It's very hard to stay on top if living with a cheater who's telling you white is black. Need clarity not the dark.

We wives did everything we could to make this situation heal. We were even more catering to the heels.

Guess I wanted him to feel how lucky he was to have me, a nut totally taking care of a worthless pig.

That he'd rather be with his computer/cheap thrills than with you. You thought it was just "adjacent offices" too.

That's the point--it's another spirit invading your home. An ugly green thing, a total invasion of your domain.

Because you don't say anything, it's gonna build. Sin escalates--it's bait as he hits bottom/you escape.

Vital energy of nurturance and care, love/time/money or emotional/sexual attention is withdrawn/gone elsewhere.

LIBERALISM IS RELAXED/NO MORALS

When you again catch him with porn don't say anything this time. Think about what it means, **REALIZE**.

The porn spirit's as bad as the Jezebel spirit in invading a home. You can feel it everywhere/no place to run.

Pornography is humiliation and degradation of women in disgraceful activity.
Noam Chomsky

LIBERAL CHIC

Written smut is as bad as visual: Porn is = writings, pictures, films used to stimulate sexual excitement.

SECRET SEX WORLD WHILE IN A RELATIONSHIP

It's a selfish sociopathic world view where the life or welfare of others is not being respected.

There's a lack of remorse/guilt, blaming others/ gaslighting and minimizing the porn: "just looked for 5 minutes".

It's a longterm pattern of disregarding and violating the rights of others. Relational conduct: ABUSIVE.

Sex addiction is marked by: a lack of control combined with significantly negative consequences.

Sex addiction despite bad effects: Having a secret sex life or WORLD while you're in a needed relationship.

The nice lady said "he said he looks at nude teens because he misses me". I laughed, it's classic minimizing.

Having a secret sex life in a family IS ABUSE since it's a selfish worldview sucking off of the host.

There's "softcore" love-story sex, incest or pseudo-incest. Tho' it's written this smut's a dark window/still a hex.

WRITTEN SMUT: EROTICA, OR "MOMMY PORN"

One result of sex addiction is deficient parenting and negligent spouse. He won't fix anything, distracted.

It's when her handsome prince becomes a disgusting weasel/it's bad when a man falls off the pedestal.

She's not just mad at him. Her whole world has been shattered. Barbara Steffans, betrayal trauma

LIBERAL CHIC

Having a secret compartmentalized sex life while in a relationship or family is in itself a form of abuse.

All the behaviors and ramifications from deception are astounding and gut-wrenching cuz she can tell it.

He's suddenly seen as a dam arrogant creep keeping THAT from me because I'm obviously an insufficiency.

There are ancillary behaviors--a cobweb--surrounding the deception--a secret world all his own, and you're gone.

In order to maintain a deceptive [secret sex] reality one tells lies--by nature be dishonest in the relationship.

They lie by omission/partial truths. That's called partial disclosure--there's always another dropping shoe.

GASLIGHTING ERODES HER REALITY

He manipulates her reality and her gut instincts which ordinarily signal truth but which he's worn down.

Maintaining a secret world while pretending to be honest--what a betrayal that is and we never coulda guessed.

The secret sexual world of one automatically ruins relational integrity, we can sense it baby.

Integrity is a major pillar in any family so if someone is chipping it away with this, see it for what it is.

Why, the chance for healthy integrity to even exist is corrupted over time--not with that goin' on.

Having a secret sexual life diverts attention away from the relationship and family. Finally, he won't do anything.

ISIS soldiers sat around watching porn all day. It leads to violence and lost affections for the finer things, ok?

LIBERAL CHIC

In all cases he has abused his wife's trust--that's in ALL cases. Porn addiction is relational abuse/rotten days.

Promises but continues to lie, be deceitful, have integrity problems, gaslight and avoid work just to lurk.

Porn is: fantasizing about anyone you are not married to.

With porn or sex addiction one takes on "life numbness" when he's out of touch with God's gloriousness.

Old psychology saw pornography as a dual addiction or a system. New psych sees wife as an abuse VICTIM.

This shift in focus away from the victim wife has done miraculous wonders for her recovery, thanks!

A BETRAYED WIFE IS AN ABUSE *VICTIM*

See the wife of the porn addict as an ABUSE victim rather than a co-conspirator {are you kidding?]

Seeing her as co-addict has ruined/killed many wives who've spent a fortune on plastic surgery for instance.

It is not due to feminism that new psychology takes the side of the porn addict's wife--it's seeing the TRUTH.

For the secret sex life of one sucks the life right out of the relationship and she knows what's up/loses trust.

Everything is intuitive in system relations and old habits are indicated thru SYMBOLS that everyone knows...

And if he has make-believe sex partners that is adultery and the wife knows something's up immediately.

A secret compartmentalized sex life is like a bubble inside the relationship, sucking all the energy into it.

LIBERAL CHIC

Instead of a vibrant colorful happy homelife, porn or affairs turns the happy home into a cold grey ghetto of strife.

A woman can tell instantly in a thousand cues. Withdrawn attention, affection, money or time to name a few.

The lady knew instantly something was up so checked his computer and there it was: more porn scum.

Porn darkens the mind, dulls the affections, disgraces the moral perspectives, brings shoddy comparisons.

Secret sex life [tho' just mental] is a bubble within a bubble. First you're a couple, now it's double/muddled.

Pornography addiction withdraws attention, affection and focus off the family and it's a real tragedy.

SECRECY IS A COMPARTMENTALIZED MISTRESS

Secrecy whether in family or politics is a compartmentalized mistress and a hex.

The nice little wifey can tell right away he's into it again and now the abuse starts as he's always plottin' and hidin'.

God made sex sacred and thus it's power. When that turns secret the home is destroyed more each hour.

It's even more erotic cuz it's secret. It's Satan's dominion as chief deceiver and your family is the ticket.

When the secret sex life is discovered the truth is finally out and the system reorganizes while going down.

He's just not into you anymore. So it's plastic surgery or sexy clothes you explore while the heart is sore.

I've written about this betrayal trauma for years for I see it as central to the frame-up in sick systems [tears].

LIBERAL CHIC

Porn is like an invading cancer sucking the elements in from the host which continues to die until lost.

Even women have porn collections now--of course they do--they're as carnal, lost and hypnotized as you.

With the invasion of porn comes the LOSS of fine art, subtle nuance, deep logic and comfy abodes.

CARTOONISH SEXUALITY OR SWEET ELEGANCE?

From small-breasted elegance to garish cartoonish sexuality everywhere and no success, it's lost.

If a woman seeks to find a "nice man" in the church she may dress just sexually enough--this is still a hex.

It's a heck of a thing with you fearing the adolescent girls who start hitting on him [or him her]--your husband.

This comes from a generational breakdown of mores: without traditional respect it becomes inappropriate.

If the man is tired, pornography gives him a "lift" from the hormone surge and that becomes addicting to elders.

He keeps me afloat, pays bills, runs errands, keeps people away and solves problems but porn is preposterous!

These are obstacles in modern computer life: the day-to-day obstructions to a nice home and a happy wife.

I know that pornography wrecks a happy homelife which is everything to me-- so I nip it in the bud, totally.

Pornography shrinks brain and experience. The lovely home seems a grey dungeon and the wife a dunce.

Codependency Therapy: If your son was hit by a truck would you want questions about his sex life?

LIBERAL CHIC

95% of the wives of sex addicts have PTSD signs. It's like a war in your house with no R & R ever--many die.

RECAP: Betrayal Trauma: a deeply distressing or disturbing experience caused by infidelity, affairs or betrayal.

HE USES SEX DISORDER TO ABUSE OTHERS

Call it SEX USE disorder: he's using sexual acting out {including porn] to abuse others. Keep this central.

It's irrelevant he's impotent. Sex addiction's about the chase leading up to the event not the two seconds.

With sex addicts the AROUSAL and excitement builds up in the planning, pursuing, searching--NOT the ending.

How is porn used to abuse me? Retribution, payback, male entitlement/dominance knowing I don't want it.

Pornography is his bubble--in his man cage--away from me, prude on the double. So it's not just the end Bro'.

Mom was always mad at Dad when he'd dance with other ladies at the Harvest Ball. That was nothing Mom.

"You'll lose the love of your life if into pornography"--if she was the love of your life, why were you into it?

Human systems so tight/interconnected that the disease of one spreads throughout: they're not just sad about it.

It has to do with early attachment trauma, secret coalitions against one and a dark evil ominous cavern.

THINK OF THE BETRAYED/TRAUMATIZED WIVES

My books are anti-feminist, not anti-women. Now I'm taking her side as she faces BETRAYAL TRAUMA.

LIBERAL CHIC

From my lovely home and starry nights with lovely sounds and beautiful sights, suddenly it was **HELL**, alright?

The sacred home was protected from evil influences but now it comes right in and we're defenseless.

Proof that it's a Sex Addiction: the negative consequences of it--loss of family and home--and he still does it.

Don't lie to me--it's secret. That's the whole point, something as disgraceful as this you lying about.

It brings down the home and the whole family. The kids can feel it and what of the pets with your divorce?

LYING: PROCRASTINATING, INCOMPLETION

He became a liar in so many ways. Like saying he'd do something then never thinking about it again.

He'd **ALWAYS** say yes he'd do it. He'd be so nice I was sure he would, tho' 1000 times he never did.

But **TRUST** is all thru the cells and soul and now that has been **SHATTERED** irrevocably/he can't see that.

It's like a bomb goes off inside. It's a shattering of everything the woman believes in/he lied.

He keeps saying "why can't we get beyond this"--it's because her reality has been shattered, that's why.

Things don't happen in a vacuum and eventually you'll pay. The effects on others are lethal like a bomb, ok?

The unexpected arrival of D-Day changes life forever as a severe rupture but you be an overcomer like others.

Porn viewing also brings perversion into the relationship and the wife must adapt. But no more, Mac.

LIBERAL CHIC

Betrayal Trauma being **TYPE ONE** brings PTSD and now the betrayed wife must deal with those symptoms.

Grafting the porn world into the intimate relationship is **INTIMACY ABUSE**. Stand your ground, you.

He must **OWN IT**: all the secrecy, the minimizing, gaslighting, tricking his wife and sneaking around.

MEN IN THERAPY KNOW THE GRAVITY

Men: You must appreciate the **IMPACT** and the **GRAVITY** of your choices because your wife has been **HURT**.

How is pornography betrayal? Intimacy Abuse: Imaginary sex partners while withdrawing from spouse.

Sex in marriage is full on emotional connection, vulnerability, love--but now it's robotic, dull, gone.

Porn: Marital love is total divine emotion, connection and love but now she's just a thing to get off.

The wife knows it, she can feel it: he's not **PRESENT**.

These men have very low **EQ**: Emotional Intelligence since they're stuck in their early trauma or when porn hit.

Not only did I trust him that much, I **RE-TRUSTED** him after serial discoveries, every time. **TRAUMA**: mine.

We ladies want a stable household--perfectly working like a Swiss watch--but mostly we want love/happiness.

It's the **TRAUMA** of loving a deceiver, Satan's other name.

Most often sex addictions starts with porn addiction.

Betrayal Trauma and consequent PTSD destroys her ability to make sense of her world. Deep trust, shattered.

LIBERAL CHIC

Away with you! I have enough to deal with in this trauma, I don't need to argue with you endlessly too.

Just when she's in the most enormous need, she can't go to him [trusted] anymore like she always did before.

The person they need the most is the person creating the trauma. And the recidivism risk is: HIGH.

The Tertiary Trauma comes soon: We're getting along but "Oh My God, Will He Do It Again?"

Even if he doesn't act out again, there's a RECIVIDISM of the Betrayal Trauma as it's triggered back up.

BEATEN UP BY THE SAME PERPETRATOR

A woman traumatized from being beaten by a stranger doesn't experience that a second time--get my line?

But the betrayed wife with deep home/family/money ties is attacked by the same perpetrator but can't get out.

The betrayed woman's job now is to move from the victim sphere into the surviving and thriving sphere.

Be ready: One husband said he didn't want to recovery. He wanted to do what he wanted and stay married.

Residual trauma: anxiety, depression, remaining out of sight, staying hypervigilant and spying on him.

The man has no idea the depth of the trauma. Really, he CAN'T know.

Difficulty concentrating or focusing, problems regulating emotions, nightmares, Why-was-I-not-enough.

Numbness, detachment, isolation from friends, insomnia, appetite gone, gut-aches, breathing problems.

LIBERAL CHIC

Betrayal trauma is a deeply heart-shattering experience. Wrong decisions are made like payback affairs.

Like all PTSD you see/hear/smell something and it brings the entire experience back. I just hate that.

If the remorseful husband can respond in a loving way, these PTSD signs can extinguish quicker.

How do we heal from Betrayal Trauma? Self-care, self-care, self-care. That's not narcissism but repair.

You are **WORTHY** of that self-care, you **DESERVE** that self-care, you will only **HEAL** from that self-care.

THE LOSER MENTALITY HAS A STINK

You are not as strong and resilient as you might think. The loser mentality will have an affect and stink.

Mom would get jealous if dad asked another woman to dance--in this generation it's far, FAR worse.

It's much more satisfying to keep tidy order, but he seemed to want a chaotic hodgepodge nightmare.

At times like this I want my mother. I'm gonna spend all day thinking of what she'd say about the messer.

PTSD is over-reactivity to sounds. Stay in small room until things become neurophysiologically normal again.

He's certainly not distinct as you are, a blazing fire. He's fuzzy, not-there, distracted, divided, a liar.

PORN AND DISORDER

You never have to point out a douche because they reveal it all by themselves.
George Bruno

LIBERAL CHIC

After a bad relationship we all realize the same thing: our family, friends and counselors all said it about him.

Betrayed wives: Look at your fears and realize he scraped the bottom of hell and brought it in to you guys.

How is pornography ABUSE? Because we're intimately tied together in a system--you're making me dirty too.

BROKEN BETRAYED WIVES, UNITE

The changed perceptions and reality living in a bombed-out city. Betrayal's as bad as THAT? REALLY?

It's the Ontologically Fatal Insight that the world isn't what you thought. Gut-aches, solar plexus hurts a lot.

Even after a five-day fast I'm still terrified in my gut. It's a primal knowing that my environment's gone to rot.

Don't feel sorry for the sinner as he goes down. This is a much bigger issue than just your little family or town.

Instead of spending time with you--his beloved wife--he prefers to sneak around looking at girlie pix and lie.

Working thru Betrayal Trauma is a PROCESS and so there is an END. Just persevere and keep talking to friends.

It's NOT about him and it's NOT about sex but about broken trust--and it LEAKS into earlier traumas.

SEX ADDICTION

It's like a leaking boat and there's nothing you can do to stop it. He swears off but back before you know it.

Most women go MAD if they are not safely ensconced in a family with a husband and children. It's freedom.

LIBERAL CHIC

Never forget, life can change very fast. Don't get complacent, by night you could have passed.

The man said "I wanted to have sex with my wife so badly and couldn't so used porn and lost her altogether."

Microaggressions: small actions or words that seem non-malicious but are felt as violence nonetheless.

The lady said "I felt sorry for him because he's old so trusted again like gold-- again he dash my hopes".

TRUST IS A FABRIC THRU EACH CELL

It's not about him, not about sex—it's about TYPE ONE TRAUMA as your world explodes in your face. KK

Betrayal is **TYPE ONE** trauma like a bombed out city. Don't wanna see anyone, don't wanna anyone to see me.

No spouse can compete with the internet. Dr. Patrick Carnes, Sex Addiction Expert

Internet Selection Mechanism: Pick a picture, up comes 100 more like what you picked then you're hooked.

JUST A CLICK: You then come into some of the deepest places sexually that people can live.

NOT ABOUT HIM/SEX BUT BROKEN TRUST

It's not about him, not about sex, it's about type one trauma as your trust in One explodes in your face.

Accessing the unresolved: he's so machine-stimulated that just one woman won't do it for him.

KIDS AND PORN: There are porn-addicts before the age of ten. We have a Tsunami coming of barbarians.

LIBERAL CHIC

Truth is ridiculed, violently rejected then accepted as what everyone knows. Three phases of Truth

Like many others, he knew better. He prosecuted others, he knew the rules-- but was still unable to stop.

What we know: arousal template has a loss of contact with reality once it's been in the reward center [AFTER].

In other words, a **LOSS OF REALITY** goes with **ADDICTION**. Despite them being very well-achieved people hon'

The addict's life is one of constant contradictions: I love my wife, but am compelled to have affairs.

Constantly telling me he loved me was the **SYMBOL** of what he was into, triggering my discovery.

All sins lay eggs called **COMPENSATIONS**. We sin, we compensate to cover it. That's how you know it.

ACROSS AMERICA HOMES ARE DESTROYED

Across the land homes are destroyed in a minute due to the powerful pull of porn on the internet.

One characteristic of the sex addict is the failure to bond. Insecure or serial attachments all unresolved.

These guys like living on the edge--part of what makes em "great". They take great risks before they are hated.

They don't have that Pursuit of Excellence. They aren't in that orderly zone doing their best in diligence.

The more you say you love me the more I know you're into pornography cuz sin's all about compensation honey.

NO WIFE CAN COMPETE WITH THE INTERNET

LIBERAL CHIC

No wife can compete with the internet if he's emotionally stuck down in early traumas unresolved.

It's a buzz, a shot of intense hormones/brain chemicals, fight or flight, hunting, the chase, early days.

Addiction is the ultimate attention deficit disorder. It puts order into things as the addict orders life around it.

If there's already ADD the addiction steps into supply that order. Our own little party alone forever.

They've shaped culture this way--sexually--and the casualty is intimacy/how they handle you and me.

He was like someone who didn't exist, sin had so warped his face. He was divided, not there, disgraced/erased.

To female genius: If he [obviously] doesn't understand you, he'll minimize/mischaracterize you too.

HIS PERSONALITY WAS SPOTTED

HE WAS EVERYTHING TO ME

Because TRUST is a fabric going thru every cell and the soul, this shattered my world but I survived to tell.

What we do affects the other person. Those closest are hidden regulators of our lives/all is known by women.

Tell a wise person or else keep silent, for the mass man will mock it right away. Guerta: The Holy Longing

The spouse of the sex addict is dealing with a broken bond, security and emotional needs are gone.

Much of the relationship feels fake like a fraud. What was her safe space leaves her disoriented and vulnerable.

WHO CAN I TRUST NOW?

LIBERAL CHIC

Who can I trust? Who will be there for me now?

She struggles alone as identity, security and stability are destroyed. Type one trauma is a shattered inner world.

All aspects of her life are affected. Creativity is shut down. Her major confidant has blown. Life sux, it's gone.

She's not in a war/bombed city but Type One Trauma is the same as if she has. Trust is a strong fabric, smashed.

Marriage is the harbor in the storm, the safe place we seek when danger presents itself in its many forms.

She feels safe in marriage then discovers danger INSIDE the marriage. Where does the betrayed go now?

It used to be just a handful of wives experienced infidelity trauma but now with internet porn it's all around ya.

ADDICTION: DESPITE MAJOR LOSSES

He lost his home, family and loving marriage just so he could watch a nude teen dance for five minutes.

He's into something big time: hormones, excitement, male entitlement--and you're just dry cuz life's a pie.

When she suddenly sees she's not the priority/there is no limbic resonance [closeness]--there's something up.

Primed by previous traumas, her nervous system lights up with his apathy: urgency, concern and distress.

Hardly anyone has worked thru major trauma or grief, so the betrayed wife is alone for no one can relate.

Her shocked grieving make them uncomfortable so they just mark her as "deeply depressed" and that's all.

LIBERAL CHIC

Friends, clergy and even therapists will put the blame back on her or minimize the Type One <u>Betrayal Trauma</u> of the hour.

PTSD can last five years. I don't remember him that much but I'll never forget that deep hell and the tears.

Suicidation is the desire to do yourself in. This with depression indicates a lack of VALIDATION.

When dealing with infidelity we're talking about the concept of HUMAN ATTACHMENT/hurts a lot.

BETRAYAL TRAUMA IS PRIMAL PANIC

Betrayal trauma [attachment distress] can bring on a PRIMAL PANIC and it's felt in the gut quick.

Human Attachments: one creates a break [porn] and the other goes into attachment distress [forlorned].

BETRAYAL TRAUMA is a deep animalistic fear that I won't be ok in the world cuz my person has betrayed me.

Primal Panic can last a long time. On the 3rd day after discovery I was high, then deep depression was mine.

In this place of gut-wrenching primal panic due to attachment distress we've lost our SAFETY.

The betrayed thinks: Am I safe? NOT--and so they become hypervigilant. Adrenalin, depression.

The Essence: I am no longer safe in this world became my person has left me in attachment distress.

After the Discovery she becomes hyper-aware of every nuance indicating abandonment and betrayal.

It's all science: Attachment Distress, Betrayal Trauma, PTSD are all Biology-- it's how it works believe me.

LIBERAL CHIC

What was the early trauma? Total dependency for food/safety on the mother lunatic, as a mammal.

Forget psychology and just be a BIOLOGIST looking at attachment distress with animals in the wilderness.

FIGHT—FLIGHT--FREEZE

The 3 responses to the trigger are fight, flight or freeze. When in fight she exacerbates the safety break.

Ok, a biological process is happening. I see my wife is impacted with adrenalin. Now, don't get defensive.

If you get defensive when she's frenetic it'll re-trigger the break in safety and create psychotic shock.

Feelings are not facts. They're just indicators of something but they drive the biological processes discussed.

The UNFIXABLE: The betrayer can't "fix" this--it is something to be endured until it is run through.

All behavior post-discovery is Safety Seeking Behavior: whether in not talking, not seeing, not touching.

Confusion and Come-Here-Go-Away: I can't be around you and feel safe/why the hell are you going away?

When the wife goes into overwhelm, when she shuts down and loses her words, you can't force her to talk jerk.

EMOTIONAL TUG OF WAR

Excruciating tug of war: She's in pain so turns to her spouse for comfort, but recoils cuz he's the culprit.

Where can she go? To a therapy group of more strangers? That makes her want her husband for comfort.

LIBERAL CHIC

There's no more reason to stay together other than financial so for that, pray to Heavenly Father.

Let's just call it an abusive unsatisfactory dynamic when we know it's wrong for us. Alan Robarge

Wake up! He's not changing and it's time you make other plans for your life. It's not working with that guy.

PAIN is the biggest motivator. Don't wanna change? Guess you haven't had enough pain yet. G. Bruno

Sinking to the depths of darkness taught us things no other way. I saw the bottom but now it's ok.

I never felt valued or appreciated for my natural gifts. He never read my work and i started to forget myself.

BETRAYAL TRAUMA SOOTHERS

When you are experiencing overwhelm, a trigger or a trauma response, go to SENSORY: MUSIC, etc.

She felt guilty for his suicidality after D Day so for two more years allowed him to abuse her with secrecy.

Lady said "I can't leave, who would take care of my dogs and cats? He's too into porn and politics to do that".

I'm not even mad at "him". This goes way beyond "him" to another world I didn't have to know about, friend.

You brain feels broken cuz the BOND was broken--attachment distress creates PRIMAL PANIC.

What is the main reason for DEPRESSION? Due to a lack of VALIDATION I don't even know myself man.

You wanna die cuz your trust has been shattered. Recognize that--it's not you it's the culprit.

LIBERAL CHIC

TRUST is like a fabric going thru every cell. BETRAYAL tears it all to hell--she feels like an empty shell.

If he's weak the man will destroy you cuz he's not strong enough to keep things away that will kill you.

BETRAYED WIFE TESTIMONY:
Journey thru a Type One Trauma

I always felt it creeping in again--a wife knows thru symbols he's not all there anymore in his sin. I thought he was one person but the spirit he's into shows he's another--a demon from hell not my brother. Thank you God for showing me light on Thanksgiving 2018. To finally accept the truth is so freeing, ultimately. You've gotta take a moral stand and see the utter disgrace of it all let alone the public shame after his fall. I can never again withstand the smut of men and I'll stay alone in withering solitude till I meet a gentleman.

My lovely home, my starry reality, my life and wisdom was SULLIED-- dirtied--by this horrible tragedy. Home life means everything to me. I banked on an illusion. I wanted peace and stability so bad I screened out reality as we both said "love ya, hon" I feel a tragic cry in my throat even as I'm writing this. Crying jags are common with the wife and kids. I feel like I've cried a river even tho' this time I didn't give in. I recall how it felt before, always terrified and cryin'

I will study betrayal trauma and broken bonds for the rest of my days. The relief already is truly amazing. So let me get this straight: you miss me so much you gotta look at nude teens. I'm finally free of this lying!

COMMENT BY A BETRAYED WIFE

The other day he said he couldn't take the trash due to a bad back. I said OK. I came back ten minutes later and he was up and about, into his porn. All day long it's politics or porn. It's these little deceptions...and what was that blanket doing in his back seat? If he wanted it for the cold, why isn't it there now? **LITTLE THINGS** like that—from partial disclosure, enough to drive you wild—put us into our **INVESTIGATIVE BEHAVIORS** which become our new illness. God help us.

TRUST AND RELATIONAL INTEGRITY AND FIDELITY

That trust is a **FABRIC** deep in the cells and soul of a woman. It is cataclysmic when that is broken. It's not about sex, it's about **LOST TRUST**. But today, even fidelity and relational integrity doesn't mean that much.

100 KAREN KELLOCK BOOKS

AFFINITY OR MISERY
AGELESS CORNUCOPIA
AMERICA AWAKE!
AMERICA'S DAFT ERA
ARTS OF PALEO FASTING
AUTOPHAGY ON CHEATERS
BACKSTABBING NEUROTICS
BETRAYAL TRAUMA
BOOMERS AND BROKENNESS
BOOT ON NECK
CHAMPION GUIDES
COMMIE NUTHOUSE
COMMIES
COMMUNIST SPIRIT
CONTAGION OF MADNESS
CONTAGIOUS MADNESS
CULTURE CLASH BASHED
DAFT LEFT
DAILY FASTARIAN
DAM RATS
DIVERSITY IS CRUELTY
E-RACE WHITE
EVIL FREAKS (Beyond Gross)
THE END OR A BEND?
FEMALE BULLIES AND FEMI-NAZIS
FEMALE CARNALITY
FEMALE DUMB DOWN
FEMALE POWER DRIVE
FEMINISM AND RUIN 1 & 2
FIX FOR MISFITS
FOOLS & TRAMPS
FREEDOM SPEAKING
FRENEMY ENABLER
FRENEMY LIAR
FRENEMY THIEF
FRENEMY TRAITOR
TRENEMY TYRANT
GENIUS IS HELD DOWN
GLOBALISLAM
GOD USES THE FLAWED
HAZE OF THE LATTER DAYS

KAREN KELLOCK PH.D.

M.S. Political Science, San Diego State. Ph.D. in Psychology, University of California Irvine. Postdoctoral: UCI School of Medicine, Dept. of Psychiatry [NIMH Grants]. Developed the Debris Theory of Disease, a theory of system pathology in 120 books and 22 textbooks for the general public. The theory has a general formula: All disease is obstruction, all recovery is elimination, all success is attraction. The three obstructions are people, habit and food. Remove obstruction and snap to your goals, waiting in the wings.